ACHIEVING FINANCIAL INDEPENDENCE AND A DEEP LOOK INTO THE LIFE OF AN IMMIGRANT.

Miguel Dos Anjos

Contents

Chapter 1: Business and Money

Chapter 2: Human Way

Chapter 3: Thirteen Years Old Entrepreneur

Chapter 4: Love Birds

Chapter 5: Baby Boy

Chapter 6: Grandpa

Chapter 7: A fighter (Grandma)

Chapter 8: Relocation

Chapter 9: New Company

Chapter 10: Brother is Born

Chapter 11: Self Defense

Chapter 12: Relocation 2

Chapter 13: Language Barrier

Chapter 14: A Healing Miracle

Chapter 15: Footsteps (Mousery)

Chapter 16: Jobs

Chapter 17: Grandpa Mass Construction

Chapter 18: Moving Spree

Chapter 19: Depression

Chapter 20: Conclusion

CHAPTER 1: BUSINESS AND MONEY

Financial independence means having enough money to keep on living without working a job. To achieve financial independence we need to create assets that will generate money. This is called Passive Income, which allows us to make money even while sleeping, be it from collecting rent on an asset or picking a stock that grows 20%.

The first step in this process is to be debt free. Starting paying off the highest interest debts first. Paying debts first, like credit cards or students loans before investing is usually the best approach, because it is hard to collect interest off an investment if somebody is collecting interest off of our debt.

Step two is to develop a 3 months security fund: $6k, more or less depending on your specific expenses. That way you have a cushing in case you decide to quit your job or an emergency arises.

Step 3 is to invest the money into assets that generate cash flow. Some assets are in the Stock Market, Real State or a business that you own and have a good manager or management team working for you.

No matter which asset, or investment we choose it is VITAL to be in a field or area that we are 100% comfortable with, and fully understand. An investment on something that somebody said was a good idea, or something we do not know or understand is a death trap.

The cash flow is all the money left over after covering expenses, generated by the assets. The cash flow can support your life expenses or it can be reinvested into new assets that will generate even more cash flow.

This reinvestment of the cash flow is the compound interest growth, if a $100 stock for example is growing at 9% rate for this cycle, it means that the next cycle you'll get the cash flow off $109 instead of the original $100 and so on. At a first look; a $9 increase may not seem like much, but investing $100 every week or month for 10 or 20 years will compound greatly. Here, time is extremely important, that's why starting this as early as possible in life is key.

Assets need to generate at least 9% interest to be a good asset, real state often times may be a little riskier than the stock market (not risk free ether), finding the right unit at the right purchase price has the potential to generate 25% or more interest, but may also at times, due to house market devaluation, cost money on the shorter run instead of generating a profit. But with time real state and the stock market goes back up. On the longer run within time it reevaluates up, being profitable again.

The worst mistake would be to sell any asset while it's undervalued. Same idea goes for the stock market; we want to buy low (on sale) and sale high. In case the market crashes the ideal path is to hold and wait for the market to pick back up, which will happen since the market is up 70% of the time.

A 3% return is what most bonds will give you but besides being a very low risk investment 3% is also the yearly average inflation. Any saved money, not generating at least 3% a year is money being lost.

All the 4 investments I mentioned so far were cash investments. One definition for "Passive Income" is income that requires work only once setting it up, and after that we can just collect. Instead of money, there are assets that require time only. A couple of good investments that can generate cash flow with time and no money are developing an online course for sale or uploading a successful monetized YouTube video for example.

All I have mentioned so far are some of the secrets to an abundant financial future. Sadly it took me to reach age 30 to come to this realization as you will see ahead.

CHAPTER 2: HUMAN WAY

Once humans started developing cities most people would be born, grow and die within 18 miles of their birth place. Amazingly, even in this more than ever, super globalized world 37 percent of the population will never live outside of their home town.

For good or bad I never had to make that choice. At age 16 I was a Brazilian teenager and dad made that choice for me. Once dad had the opportunity to go to the USA he did not think twice.

Dad always told me; "My son, face the world with a wide open chest", in Portuguese that saying always made so much more sense. Anyways, the idea he wanted me to understand was to never be afraid, always take calculated risks and aim as high as possible. And that is what he always did.

CHAPTER 3: THIRTEEN YEARS OLD ENTREPRENEUR

For dad no obstacle was big enough to scare him away. In a family of 6 siblings it was always a good idea to keep eyes wide open and see things first. Grandpa, on my father side, was a retired military man, which was a great thing for the time. It meant status and a certain degree of good conditions. Misery and starvation was not the case, which is great considering the conditions in Brazil. Still, all that, certainly did not mean everything was rainbows.

At age thirteen dad started working in construction. With the money coming in he bought himself a bicycle and kept that going for a while, at that point the concept of getting things done on his own had started, after all why wait for somebody to do for him what he could do himself – made a lot of sense, but personally, call me soft, at age thirteen that was not in my mind.

At age 17, dad was almost done with high school and at that same time the construction business was booming, dad started working in the richest area of our state (Minas Gerais). The Savaci location was where the money was. At that point he started realizing that he could get, and lock in jobs that would pay more than in poorer areas. Also, hiring other people to get the work done for him would allow him to finish projects much faster, and even take multiple jobs simultaneously. Dad would then be the head contractor and delegate work to other 3 of his employees.

While all that happened during the day, at night dad would go back to school, but at that point he would everyday miss the first and sometimes the second classes of the school nights. Then, watch two classes, and then end up sleeping the last class due to exhaustion at the end of an 18 hours daily journey. Don't be afraid, none of that was a problem for dad, lack of sleep never bothered him. Two years later; high school diploma in hands, the world was the limit, he even met the math teacher from the first class on graduation day.

CHAPTER 4: LOVE BIRDS

As you've seen buying a bike at thirteen, working, saving and running a company was some of dad's accomplishments but his vision was farther ahead. Nonetheless smoking and evening cocktails definitely helped put thoughts and things together. By the way when I say cocktails don't get too fancy thinking of cosmopolitans, manhattans or margaritas, too expensive, too fancy, non existent. It mostly meant rum and beers, and the really good beers were, and still are just two of them, "Brahma" and "Skol". But I won't lie caipirinhas we did, and do have, similar to a mojito, really, really great!

Anyway as I was saying the place to meet new people was the Avenida Vilarinho (the main avenue in Venda Nova). Everyone got together and had a great time, shish kebab, French fries and shrimp portions were some of the most famous. And there, one night, dad now 20 years old, had already turned the bicycle into a real bike, met mom, also 20 years old. A young lady also coming from a family of 6 siblings, similar stories. Love was in the air. They had a great night, so great that three months later the decision was made; MERIAGE.

Before going to the court house mom told dad; "hey babe, three months might seem to the court house people that we could be moving too fast. Let's tell them that we've been together for 6 months instead." Dad says; "oh great, that'll be good". Once inside the courthouse, the question comes up; "how long you've been together?",

Mom; "6 months"

Agent; "6 MONTHS?" shocked.

Mom; "what? Is that too much?"

After getting married finding a place to live was a harder task. In Brazil if a land owner does not use his land, making it productive, and leave it doing nothing and somebody else comes and claims that piece of land; there is a chance that person keeps that land. They found a piece of land, a block away from the slum, sadly there is no escape from slums in Brazil. Wherever a rich city gets built the poor people come and build a slum. Often times, right next to a big city searching for the opportunities a big provides.

Dad quickly built a house. Soon after, the land owner shows up, yes, the land wasn't being productive but mom and dad were offered two choices; (1) leave and lose all they had built in the land, or (2) buy the land from the owner, that way keeping all they had already invested in the house. None of the choices were great, but buying the land seemed and was the best option.

Each of my parents working daily 16 hours shifts paid for the land, finished building and expending the house. Then they decided it was time to grow the family. Mom got pregnant, but she had just had turned 20, and was still somewhat young, holding two teaching jobs, plus loads of stress. Mom had a miscarriage early in the pregnancy. Extremely sad for mom, and my older (brother to be), due to those facts a second try happened and I came to be. Today when I look at it I feel so sad for my brother but at the same time I'm so happy to have been given a chance to appreciate this world and due the hard circumstances there wasn't much of a chance for my parents to choose to have 2 children back then. In reality the way I see it, there was barely conditions to have even one child, but the most important they had; loving and

Achieving Financial Independence and a Deep Look Into the Life of an Im-caring.

CHAPTER 5: BABY BOY

I don't remember much, but it was probably one of the happiest days of my life, being born, or maybe not. Definitely not for mom, you see, the circumstances were hard. Mom 9 months waiting for me and the water brakes! The hospital was super far - money for cab? - there was none. Mom catches a bus. At the hospital they decided to do natural birth. The nurse asks; "miss would you like anesthesia?", once again, the budget was small to none at all. "What do you mean? Money for anesthesia?" At that point mom might have thought: "that nurse must be joking".

I have a feeling all this was part of the reason I was an only child for 13 years.

Thanks to grandma baby me had 4 covers for that Brazilian July winter season. All my four covers were made from one old adult blanket that grandma and mom managed to cut in 4. I don't fully remember it, but whenever I try to look back I imagine a lovely set of 4 blue blankets that kept me warm that winter and possibly another 4 or 5 more winters later.

Time flew by. Once I turned 4 I started having my first memories that I could keep the rest of my life. Our house built by dad was so big. We had a gigantic land, so big specially throw the eyes of a 4 to 6 years old. In the front yard there was a mango tree and a guava tree, and in the back yard we had an avocado tree and a banana field with what looked like to me 5 to 6 banana trees, but my grandparents would swear to me that, that was only one banana tree because what seemed to be 5 trees to me was actually connected and together belonged to one tree. How would I argue with adults? In reality I didn't even feel the need to. Whatever they would say to me I thought was true and the only true.

Crazy funny grandpa would take advantage of how much I admired how knowledgeable the adults were, and since I would believe anything they'd tell me he would at times play jokes on me like when he taught me how to use the car's seat belt wrapping it around my neck 3 times before clicking it. Taking all in consideration, when I look back today, why on earth did I just accept that as the true. I guess it just shows how much of a roll ignorance can play.

CHAPTER 6: GRANDPA

All grandpa's jokes aside. Grandpa along with grandma were also my godparents. They had 6 daughters, my 5 aunts and my mother. I was their first grandson, they loved me and showered me with love.

Maybe the reason sometimes I forget how crazy it was to have dad start working at 13 years of age, might have to do with grandpa starting to work at 6 years of age. Grandpa was born far away in the farmland and did not have the chance to finish school.

By age 6 he had to prepare the land for the seeds, plant the seeds, etc, etc,.. While doing all that I remember how he used to tell me how bad it was with the mosquitos that would not leave him alone. So he was taught a trick; if he lit up a cigar the smoke would keep the mosquitos away, which, does make sense. Why would a mosquito want to stay close to that cigar's smoke, the mosquito could catch a cancer or something.

Going this much far in the past plus a far away location, there was no such thing as money. They would trade milk for grains, or whatever was in the season and they could afford to trade for something else they didn't have.

By age 20 all grandpa's only valuable possession was one baby pig that after being healthily fed for many months turned into a huge pig. What did grandpa do? He sold his only valuable and bought his first pairs of shoes, on his 20's for the first time grandpa was not barefoot. With all the left over money grandpa bought a train ticket to Belo Horizonte, the capital of our state. There grandpa met grandma, got a job, married grandma, had their 6 daughters and built a total of 5 houses.

    No doubt grandpa was my second father. Their struggle was real. How could I ever complain about anything after thinking about how they had had it?!

CHAPTER 7: A FIGHTER (GRANDMA)

Grandma had a high school diploma and was a home wife, which I'm sure was a lot of hard work, especially after having 6 daughters, at times I wonder how grandpa felt having 7 women in the house. When grandma's second oldest daughter, my mother, finished high school and went to college grandma decided to join.

All 6 daughters, and now grandma as well, attended college and they all got education degrees. The catch was that in Brazil anyone can go to college if you can pay for it. Imagine how crazy it would be to pay for college for 7? That was certainly not an option, so, plan B it was, which was going to public school which was the far better education anyone could get as a result of all the recourses that would then be available. The problem was and is that to qualify for a public university the candidates had to pass the test (known by locals as "vestibular") with top scores, and thankfully after lots of studying and God's blessing 7 education degrees were obtained.

While catching up, and doing all that grandma did; due to some lung complication earlier in her life she had lost one third of her lungs, which we could never tell, apart from an occasional loss of breath.

Sadly after many years passed by, around grandma's 80's it had finally caught up to her. Many of us thought there was something going on with grandma's brain due to her way of thinking. Finally one day, extremely late in the process, a doctor reached the correct diagnose and realized the amount of carbon dioxide in grandma's body was too high, lacking enough oxygen in the brain, thus debilitating her thinking and thought process to a certain degree.

CHAPTER 8: RELOCATION

By age 6 dad decided we could do better than a house 2 blocks away from a slum. The fact our house had been robed 3 times might have played a role in that decision.

Which was hard to image, why were people robing us? We were poor too.

No complains, after selling a house to a foreigner from Sao Paulo and cashing in some money, we bought an apartment in Belo Horizonte, our state's capital. A great jump upwards.

Looking at my new neighbors, at first I felt I didn't belong, and that they were rich, but as time passed by we really felt we belonged, not to mention, some of our new capital neighbors were lawyers and doctors and definitely had prestige and made money, but still had to work and provide services equally as my parents did. Mom in the education field and dad self-employed.

On the other side some of our new neighbors, besides been in a richer area seemed to have the same struggles as our old neighbors in that poorer area. At that point I started realizing no matter where we were people were just people.

CHAPTER 9: NEW COMPANY

As time passed by, dad, then on his 30s, he decided to go for a change, and become a sales man. It felt that dad would never work for somebody else besides his own self.

Dad changed everything construction and building related to a small truck where he then made sales and delivered himself. I was then 11 years old and many times dad would take me. It was a great opportunity to learn some of the skills of a sales person. I would really, really love it, and be so happy to have dad share his way of thinking with me. At the time I could fully realize what he was saying, not at all times I would agree with what he would say. There was no need for me to tell him that ever though, if at any point I showed I had doubts on his thought processing it could give him a sign not to explain or share with me. And believe me, what he taught me, was not rocket science, it was often saying things that the customer wanted to hear, was being a decent human being, or just saying something that would improve or up the sell. At any point there was any wrong tricks, because if for any reason the customer wanted to or had to, they could return the merchandise, plus, dad returned every week to resupply the customer and collect last week paying from last sold products. Keeping a healthy relation was ideal.

At times if the costumer was a bigger corporation, posing a picture that we were bigger and dealt with huge sales would be good. At the same time when dealing with a more humble customer or selling house, posing a more humble picture of himself would also be helpful.

At the end of the day the biggest part into being successful dealing with people was probably to like people and have them like you. That way, they would look at the merchandise, all around, in a better environment. Furthermore I did mention that at times I didn't fully agree with dad way of doing certain things, that did not matter, because the most import thing he had was confidence. No matter what he was doing or believed was the right approach he would do it with certainty that he had made the best choice, no doubts, no confusion, just developing a plan and following throw.

CHAPTER 10: BROTHER IS BORN

A couple of years later mother got pregnant with my younger brother.

My parents were super nice and let me choose his name, me a 13 year old, his first name was great; Vitor, which translates to Victor and means "victory". The bad turn happens now, I didn't know better, and gave him 4 more names after that. At times that becomes confusing, I wish I could take 2 or 3 of his names away. My younger brother was to me the son I have never had, loved and still love him with all my heart. A few nights with no sleep at the first year did bother me, but what on earth does not bother a teenager.

My brother has become one my prides, with all his success and achievements plus a full scholarship to a top university.

CHAPTER 11: SELF DEFENSE

When I was age 15 an opportunity came to dad. To go to the USA for a year, maybe 2 to 3 years and for the first time he would be working for another person that was not him. Even though, a little hard, he decided to go for it.

When he left, my younger brother was 1. It must have been super hard for dad to leave all behind. Often times I would miss dad. It did not feel good not having dad around, to me dad was a superhero, a big man, who would be there for protection whenever needed. That protection was many times emotional, but in Brazil there are many real dangers as well. It helped greatly having grandpa, and the church pastor around who always provided good advices to be good, honest people and follow a good path.

Being skinny and young I felt vulnerable, and decided to join the self-defense gym to improve my abilities of defending myself, also after being robed another 3 times. Two of those times I had not realized I had been robbed until much later when I had reached into my book bag for my wallet.

In a big city many times people bump into you, and waiting for the pedestrian crossing light somebody bumped into me. I was a 16 years old; "how much money could a 16 year old have in

Brazil?" Once again the poor robing the poor. I kept going with my life walking to the bus stop. Never realized anything. Once I'm inside the bus reaching for the wallet to get the ticket to pay the bus I realized what had happened, ... those sneaky thieves!!! ...

After joining the gym and training 3 hours a days, 5 days a week. I had improved my cardio vascular system and developed many good skills, that would stay with me for the rest of my life. Physical skills, also mental skills.

Two years later training that intensely, I also developed an over use of the knee's cartilage. I went to the doctor thinking he would give me a pill and all would be back to normal again, but the doctor told me to do more stretching before exercising and to do some legs focused weight training to make the leg muscles stronger and take some of the hard work being imposed on the knees. All the doctor advices helped but that was it; "helped" didn't fully, or magically instantly cure my knees. My hopes and expectation were done for doctors. Until that situation I fully believed doctors could cure and heal us. But the doctor sits me down explains to me, we cannot just go right away operate on you, we have to give it time, and take in consideration if the benefits out-weight the risks. I fully understood what the doctor said, still, my frustration was gigantic. With that much pain, after 2 years of training, I knew that was it for me, I would never be able to fully practice martial arts again going through that much knee pain.

CHAPTER 12: RELOCATION 2

At age 18; by now dad is completing 3 years in the USA as a construction worker.

The plans then changed a bit. At that point dad had been in the USA from 2000 to 2003. The USA economy was good. A great time to be in any field, for sure any type of construction field: bricks, blocks, carpentry, painting, etc. Being 3 years family separated was very sad to all parts, me, dad, mom and my younger brother that was then 1 year old who had now turned 4.

My parents started working into reuniting the family in the USA and so they did. Dad would work for a company that was a contractor getting projects from the government to build and expend schools. Mom, left her school position then, as a Middle School vice principle, and had become a pre-k teacher in a bilingual community.

CHAPTER 13: LANGUAGE BARRIER

That bilingual community was great for me. I had the chance to actually learn English, even though I had been taking English 1, 2 and 3 back in Brazil. School seemed to always start every year back at the verb TO BE.

At the time I was never sure if I should blame the teachers, the system, or the students. I did get that question answered once I realized nobody could learn a new language for me and I would need to learn it myself and to reach any positive goals the faster I learned it the better.

Mom bought me a small dictionary and I would keep it in my pocket, I would use it so often that after 2 months whenever I needed to figure out a word's meaning I would instantly open the dictionary on the page that the word was located. Sadly for me many times I'd get frustrated not finding the word I wanted because it was a slang like "ain't" or somebody's name like "Carolina" and the worse of all trying to translate word by word instead of a full sentence would often times leave me thinking that "imsorry" or "excuseme" were one word and not a combination of two or three words. It was a challenging and rough first 2 months.

On top of that, even though, not everybody realizes it, Brazilians do not speak Spanish. Spanish and Portuguese certainly have many similarities. Taking away a speaker accent and pronunciation, one third of Portuguese and Spanish words are the same or almost the same and another one third of the words are the same, but with a different meanings.

All around me there were so many Spanish speakers, that it became a great opportunity to pick up a third language. Now fluent in English, Portuguese and Spanish I finished high school, went to college and decided to take my first official Spanish class where I could improve writing skills and get deeper into a more proper grammar. The college after studying my case decide to skip me ahead to intermediate Spanish.

CHAPTER 14: A HEALING MIRACLE

Healthy once again, still young, I joined a new martial arts gym under a new instructor.

After around one year, miraculously my knees had fully recovered. That's when I learned not to underestimate the power of "giving it time". That lesson would sadly be needed again later.

After thinking that my knee injury would never allow me back at the gym I recovered, two more years in, and my lower back started giving me problems. I guess I took so much care of my knees that I forgot about protecting the lower back. Once again the same doctors that had already disappointed me once manage to disappoint me again. Doctors never seemed to have a fix it quick pill to give me.

The doctor told me I needed more stretching, and that I had over used my back muscles and tendons, I had to give it a couple of weeks to recover, then do longer warm ups, etc, etc. Facing that much pain there was no way I would ever be able to train again, or so I thought.

The pain was excruciating, but a year, full 12 painful months, later it went away, by now I had experienced pain in every part of the body, bruises weren't the worse, those healed quicker. Longer term joints over use were a much bigger issue.

Back at it a second time, after crying thinking the end had come. A second healing miracle happened and I was back at the gym. Many times at moments the body capabilities makes us feels super humans, but experience had already showed me, twice, to never abuse the one body God's given us.

Collecting trophies from competitions was always gratifying and self-steaming boosting.

On competitions I would get lots of first and second places for the patters where all competitors often 10 to 20 separated by ranks only, would compete doing elimination rounds, based on a 5 referee score judging.

For the sparring / fighting; competitors would get split often in smaller groups taking in consideration, age, weight and ranks. While in the lower rank belts fights were extremely easy to me. I had had a great background back home.

Although different from some people I loved to know self-defense. One of the first self-defense lessons is to not need to use it. Good judgment allows one to realize a threat in the making before it happens. Be it a stranger crossing a street late at night clearly coming to you, or a friend or somebody that we know, that had too many drinks become challenging. Following lesson one, and maybe together with some luck, more often than not, there's no need to even get to lesson two.

Lesson two is not too complex either. Not being able to avoid the situation or threat; now already fully inside the action DO NOT wait to get punched or stabbed to react. That will be too late, this is the reason the same technic is practiced thousands of times, boring? Yes. But now the technic becomes part of you. While some people can take a punch I could not. This is why it is crucial to react before the opponent comes close enough to become a real threat or even touches you.

Third; worst case scenario. It's too late. You might have your head locked under somebody's arm, about to pass out due to lack of oxygen. This is when; it has hit the fan. Time to reach into the knowledge tool box. Depending on the situation, your back head hit to the offender's nose or thumbs on pressure points such as; nose, eyes, throat, groins for example are usually great to allow a lock to come to an end. Followed up by a knee or elbow, should be a job accomplished.

These two steps are usually enough to create enough time for you to walk away or call the cops. There is never need to keep at it. If you're spending time reading a book and being productive means that; the person on the ground is in another level, he or she will not play by the same rules. While you and I care about our futures, the biggest chance is that such a person has nothing to lose, no good job, or a clean record. No need to prove anything to anybody. You will thank yourself later for having a cool mind during that high stakes moment and walk away avoiding headaches.

Tournaments were none of that. I never hurt or wanted to hurt anybody, I always aimed at scoring points. After all a competitor was somebody just like me, with so many more similarities than not. Competing under lower level belts and ranks was extremely easy and fun. Things changed at the higher levels.

That's when I realized most competitors did not reach a red or black belt by chance. By definition red means; danger. A red belt and a black belt individual will know the same technics, the difference is that a black belt will have much more control. And a red belt can hurt somebody, even without the intention to do so for lack of full control.

For mister nice guy over here competitions had reached the real deal. Aiming at scoring points alone would not cut it at such levels. Bad intentions would be disqualifying in a competition but the need to tire the opponent was very real.

Any ways, all together, it was 10 years of training. I had to definitely push it throw to reach the black belt and Instructor title, after not once but twice thinking the dream was over.

CHAPTER 15: FOOTSTEPS (MOUSERY)

Around my early teens feeling I was behind in life compared to grandpa and dad I decided to raise some money myself. I had a few Chinese hamsters' pets, and I realized with proper care they could make me some money.

Putting a male and female together they would go about their business and that was the first step.

After that I had to separate them (the hamster couple), there is a chance the father will not be of any help with the babies. A clean, safe ideal environment is needed for the female to feel well with no stress to raise a healthy litter. No rocket science; adequate food, clean water, some privacy is all it took the mom hamster. Three to four weeks later the babies grew and needed to be separated by males and females to prevent inbreeding or early pregnancies.

Following those rules and a few more I managed to keep 4 litters at all times been raised.

In Brazil there was not much regulation going at that time for a small Chinese hamster pet. Once a month I would take the 4 week litters to the pet store and sell him my hamsters 2.5 Reais

(Brazilian money) at the time per hamster, each litter had usually 7 to 8 hamsters. That money felt great in my wallet, got me a new bike and a few clothes. In reality I had always loved animals, so much that raising pets was in itself super satisfying, profit was just a bonus.

CHAPTER 16: JOBS

At age 18 I started doing a variety of part time jobs. Part time positions were great for a little income, while an individual does not yet hold a vast quantity of experience in a specific field. Still, I wish I knew then, what I know today.

It is extremely hard to become financially well off exchanging time for money, because there is a locked amount of hours in each day. An individual can only work 15 to 20 hours a day maximum, which is already not healthy or sustainable on the long run, so the only way to save a vast amount of wealth for a rainy day or for the future would be to become extremely experienced in an area and have your time be paid highly. Since most positions can easily be replaceable and having a skill that only you know is hard to find or obtain, the easier way to be well off in the future is to invest in assets.

Many times people confuse assets with liabilities. Assets will be any source of income one has while a liability will drain money from your bank account. A house will be an asset if you rent it, and the rent pays for all its costs like; mortgage and insurance and you still have a cash flow coming.

Went to High School Monday to Friday, and on weekends and vacations would work on construction. Nothing too big, at times assisting my high school math teacher that hired me by the hour to help him redoing his house floor or using other friend connections to hire me for the day for specific projects. Another short time opportunity was house / mansions cleaning, mostly vacuuming all day huge mentions. Extremely fun to see what life was to some better off people but I would never dream, then, to reach that far up.

Once in college I had been given a much more flexible schedule so I got hired by a warehouse in the immigrant area I lived in, to operate fork-lifts and jack-pallets on the night shift. Once I showed up to work around 3 pm I would be given a block of papers. Each page was the list order of products a specific customer wanted. All night moving pallets up and down and at the end of the night loading all pick up orders into the appropriate trucks in addresses' order for next morning delivery.

Almost two years, too long, having fun driving the warehouse jack-pallets and fork-lifts, also too dangerous, every month an employee would leave their feet in between jack pallets, or a high up grocery pallet would fall down.

It was time for a little upgrade. A friend of mine in college that I met in a C++ programing class, brought me to work with him as a buzzer in a fine dining restaurant in the Tribeca area in Manhattan. Once again I had the chance to watch rich people live their lives. Funny that mom had always told me not to put my elbows on the table while eating, and use the fork and knife properly, or mind how loud my voice tone was. That was not the case for those people, especially the one's ordering from the $4k wine bottles list. For the most part they could not care less about minor things happening around them. Being the buzz boy or food runner serving food from the left side of guests, and the coffee guy; making macchiatos and Americanos was interesting.

CHAPTER 17: GRANDPA MASS CONSTRUCTION

Once in the capital, no longer farming and finally using money, instead of trading eggs for milk grandpa bought a piece of land and built a house. Already with grandma and growing the family they built a second, bigger house moved in and transformed the first house into a private school for younger children.

As time passed by, a third house was built. The family then, moved into that house and now had two units available for rent.

From what grandpa had seen and learned in his early days, he did his absolute best. Eventually, a few more land investments, he built 3 more houses.

As age and time came. Managing all that became more and more complex, specially after grandma's passing. Slowly all was sold and passed on to the children.

CHAPTER 18: MOVING SPREE

At age 0 to 6 we lived in an invaded piece of land that eventually my parents had to pay for it.

Eventually we moved to a better area and rented the house. Every two years the lease would end, and we would need to move again until one day dad sold that first house he built and bought a new one in the capital.

A few years later dad moved to the USA, 3 more years passed, and he brought me, mom and my little brother to be with him.

CHAPTER 19: DEPRESSION

Around age 18 I had 1000 plans. By age 24 I would have a 4 years degree, a job on that field, be married, have a child. I turned 24, none of those things had come to reality. I had a 2 years degree could not find a job on my field due to multiple circumstances. Nonetheless I decided to keep pushing throw and kept working towards my goals and I felt and hoped that if I kept at it, all would come true.

In reality, just because we want something or even work towards getting it, alone, that does not mean it will be achieved or that we would be entitled to it.

By age 26, two years later, nothing seemed to be going my way. Sadness started coming in, I was going into a deep depression with so much disappointment.

Thankfully to God, I kept planning. A couple of times I felt it was too much work, and none of my dreams were coming true. That's when I would drop on my knees and ask God to open my eyes, help me see the best path, and approach, because clearly as a mere human being I had not yet seen the bigger picture.

But then, a few more months in, things started happening. I reached the martial arts Instructor Assistant black belt after twice being severely diagnosed with extreme knees and lower back joints over use. Over $40k and 8 years I finally got an IT bachelor's degree. Developed 4 programs which led many companies to take deep looks into me, never for one moment I regret getting education, but after being offered opportunities in a less demanding field with benefits things finally seemed to be moving in a good direction.

CHAPTER 20: CONCLUSION

At times I hear people say rich people are bad or that people who have money only think about money and are materialist. That is a self-sabotaging way of thinking. If we believe or imagine something being bad we will never get there. A rich person does not have to be a bad person. Most rich people who reach the top climbing their own selves instead of inheriting it, worked hard early on their lives, and not necessarily stole from somebody else to get to the top.

The only way to get to the top and keep being there is to want to get and be there, and set up a plan to achieve it. Most people we ask if they would like to be a millionaire, they will say: "Yes, of course I want to be a millionaire!", but will never do anything to get there. In such case; even if they win the lottery and become a millionaire they don't stay there because they spend all the money on liabilities instead of assets that can keep the money growing.

For example this is the case we see for so many super rich young star that become broke again after having made millions, because they were born poor and never learned or educated themselves into investing and developing assets. That's why being rich is often times considered a "state of mind". The right state of mind allows people to become rich once again, even in the event of losing everything.

Don't wait for tomorrow or next year to start. If financial freedom is what you want, act and plan today, set achievable short term goals, also medium and long term goals. The power of compound interest is real. My only regret is not having started earlier.

Best of luck!

www.ingramcontent.com/pod-product-compliance
Lightning Source LLC
Chambersburg PA
CBHW030738180526
45157CB00008BA/3226